One Family's Story
A Primer on Bowen Theory

Michael E. Kerr, MD

Bowen Center for the Study of the Family
Georgetown Family Center

Washington, DC

Bowen Center for the Study of the Family
Georgetown Family Center
   4400 MacArthur Boulevard NW, Suite 103
   Washington, DC 20007-2521

   www.thebowencenter.org

Edited by: Ruth Riley Sagar
Designed by: Elizabeth M. Utschig

ISBN 0-9658540-2-7

Library of Congress Control Number: 2002116266

Printed in the United States of America

Preface

One Family's Story: A Primer on Bowen Theory is being published to provide a convenient and affordable way for people to have access to a comprehensive description of Bowen theory.

Originally written for the Bowen's Center website, the idea to publish the Bowen theory section in booklet form originated when a faculty member who directs a family crisis center suggested that Dr. Kerr's description of the theory would be very useful to the people his center served. His comments, coupled with the realization that the Bowen theory section had been far and away the most popular feature on our website, led to the decision to publish the Primer.

Dr. Kerr takes a new approach to presenting the eight concepts in an effort to make the theory more easily understood to a wide audience, many of whom will be learning about theory for the first time. He recounts the story of a fictional family to describe and explain each concept.

It is hoped that *One Family's Story* will bring the theory alive for all who read it and will encourage them to pursue the benefits of applying it in their own lives.

Special acknowledgement is extended to Dr. Murray Bowen whose observations and ideas led to the development of Bowen family systems theory on which *One Family's Story* is based and to Dr. Michael Kerr and the other faculty of the Bowen Center whose endeavors have lead to increased knowledge about the human family as an adapting, evolving part of all life.

Ruth Riley Sagar
March 2003
Washington, DC

IV

Also published by the Georgetown Family Center

Bowen Theory and Practice

The Emotional Side of Organizations

Family Systems: A Journal of Natural Systems
Thinking in Psychiatry and the Sciences

Understanding Organizations

Contents

Introduction

Bowen family systems theory is a theory of human behavior that views the family as an emotional unit and uses systems thinking to describe the complex interactions in the unit. It is the nature of a family that its members are intensely connected emotionally. Often people feel distant or disconnected from their families, but this is more feeling than fact. Families so profoundly affect their members' thoughts, feelings, and actions that it often seems as if people are living under the same "emotional skin." People solicit each other's attention, approval, and support and react to each other's needs, expectations, and upsets. The connectedness and reactivity make the functioning of family members interdependent. A change in one person's functioning is predictably followed by reciprocal changes in the functioning of others. Families differ somewhat in the degree of interdependence, but it is always present to some degree.

The emotional interdependence presumably evolved to promote the cohesiveness and cooperation families require to protect, shelter, and feed their members. Heightened tension, however, can intensify these processes that promote unity and teamwork, and this can lead to problems. When family members get anxious, the anxiety can escalate by spreading infectiously among them. As anxiety goes up, the emotional connectedness of family members becomes more stressful than comforting. Eventually, one or more members feels overwhelmed, isolated, or out of control. These are the people who accommodate the most to reduce tension in others. It is a reciprocal interaction. For example, a person takes too much responsibility for the distress of others in relationship to their unrealistic expectations of him, or a person gives up too much control of his thinking and decision-making in relationship to others anxiously telling him what to do. The one who does the most accommodating literally "absorbs" system anxiety and thus is the family member most vulnerable to problems such as depression, alcoholism, affairs, or physical illness.

Dr. Murray Bowen, a psychiatrist, originated this theory and its eight interlocking concepts. He formulated the theory by using systems thinking to integrate knowledge of the human species as a product of evolution with knowledge from family research. A core assumption is that an emotional system that evolved over several billion years governs human relationship systems. People have a "thinking brain," language, a complex psychology and culture, but people still do all the ordinary things other forms of life do. The emotional system affects most human activity and is the principal driving force in the development of clinical problems. Knowledge of how the emotional system operates in one's family, work, and social systems reveals new and more effective options for solving problems in each of these areas.

Triangles

A *triangle* is a three-person relationship system. It is considered the building block or "molecule" of larger emotional systems because a triangle is the smallest stable relationship system. A two-person system is unstable because it tolerates little tension before involving a third person. A triangle can contain much more tension without involving another person because the tension can shift around three relationships. If the tension is too high for one triangle to contain, it spreads to a series of "interlocking" triangles. Spreading the tension can stabilize a system, but nothing gets resolved.

People's actions in a triangle reflect their efforts to assure their emotional attachments to important others, their reactions to too much intensity in the attachments, and their taking sides in others' conflicts. Paradoxically, a triangle is more stable than a dyad, but a triangle creates an odd man out, which is a very difficult position for individuals to tolerate. Anxiety generated by anticipating being or by being the odd man out is a potent force in triangles.

The patterns in a triangle change with increasing tension. In calm periods, two people are comfortably close "insiders" and the third person is an uncomfortable "outsider." The insiders actively exclude the outsider, and the outsider works to get closer to one of them. Someone is always uncomfortable in a triangle and pushing for change. The insiders solidify their bond by choosing each other in preference to the less desirable outsider. When someone chooses another person over oneself, it arouses particularly intense feelings of rejection.

If mild to moderate tension develops between the insiders, the most uncomfortable one will move closer to the outsider. One of the original insiders now becomes the new outsider and the original outsider is now an insider. The new outsider will make predictable moves to re-store closeness with one of the insiders. At moderate tension levels, triangles usually have one side in conflict and two harmonious sides. The conflict is not inherent in the relationship in which it exists, but reflects the overall functioning of the triangle.

At a high level of tension, the outside position becomes the most desirable. If severe conflict erupts between the insiders, one insider opts for the outside position by getting the current outsider fighting with the other insider. If the maneuvering insider is successful, he gains the more comfortable position of watching the other two people fight. When the tension and conflict subside, the outsider will try to regain an inside position.

Triangles contribute significantly to the development of clinical problems. For example, getting pushed from an inside to an outside position can trigger a depression or perhaps even a physical illness, or two parents intensely focusing on what is wrong with a child can trig-ger serious rebellion in the child.

Example

Michael and Martha were extremely happy during the first two years of their marriage. Michael liked making major decisions, and Martha felt comforted by Michael's "strength." After some difficulty getting pregnant, Martha conceived during the third year of the mar-riage, but it was a difficult pregnancy. She was quite nauseous during the first trimester and developed blood pressure and weight gain prob-lems as the pregnancy progressed. She talked frequently to Michael of her insecurities about being a mother. Michael was patient and reas-suring, but also began to feel critical of Martha for being "childlike."

Analysis: The pregnancy places more pressure on Martha and on the marital relationship. Michael is outwardly supportive of Martha, but is reactive to hearing about her anxieties. He views her as having a problem.

A female infant was born after a long labor. They named her Amy. Martha was exhausted and not ready to leave the hospital when her doctor discharged her. Over the next few months, she felt increasingly overwhelmed and extremely anxious about the well-being of the young baby. She looked to Michael for support, but he was getting home from the office later and Martha felt he was critical of her coping problems and that he dismissed her worries about the child. There was much less time together for just Michael and Martha and, when there was time, Michael ruminated about work problems. Martha became increasingly preoccupied with making sure her growing child did not develop the insecurities she had. She tried to do this by being as attentive as she could to Amy and consistently reinforcing her accomplishments. It was easier for Martha to focus on Amy than it was for her to talk with Michael. She reacted intensely to his real and imagined criticisms of her. Michael and Martha spent more and more of their time together discussing Amy rather than talking about their marriage.

Analysis: Martha is the most uncomfortable with the increased tension in the marriage. The growing emotional distance in the marriage is balanced by Martha getting overly involved with Amy and Michael getting overly involved with his work. Michael is in the outside position in the parental triangles and Martha and Amy are in the inside positions.

As Amy grew, she made increasing demands on her mother's time. Martha felt she could not give Amy enough time, that Amy would never be satisfied. Michael agreed with Martha that Amy was too selfish and resented Amy's temper tantrums when she did not get her way. However, if Michael got too critical of Amy, Martha would defend Amy, telling Michael he was exaggerating. Yet, whenever tensions developed between Martha and Amy, Martha would press Michael to spend more time with Amy to reassure her that she was loved. He gave into Martha's pleas, but inwardly felt that they were following a policy of appeasement that was making Amy more demanding. Michael felt that if Martha had his maturity, Amy would be less of a problem, but, despite this attitude, Michael usually followed Martha's lead in relationship to Amy.

Analysis: When tension builds between Martha and Amy, Michael sides with Martha by agreeing that Amy is the problem. The conflictual side of the triangle then shifts from between Martha and Amy to between Michael and Amy. If the conflict gets too intense between Michael and Amy, Martha sides with Amy, the conflict shifts into the marriage, and Amy gains the more comfortable outside position.

Differentiation of Self

Families and other social groups tremendously affect how people think, feel, and act, but individuals vary in their susceptibility to a groupthink and groups vary in the amount of pressure they exert for conformity. These differences between individuals and between groups reflect differences in people's levels of *differentiation of self*. The less developed a person's "self," the more impact others have on his functioning and the more he tries to control, actively or passively, the functioning of others. The basic building blocks of a "self" are inborn, but an individual's family relationships during childhood and adolescence primarily determine how much "self" he develops. Once established, the level of "self" rarely changes unless a person makes a structured and long-term effort to change it.

People with a poorly differentiated "self" depend so heavily on the acceptance and approval of others that either they quickly adjust what they think, say, and do to please others or they dogmatically proclaim what others should be like and pressure them to conform. Bullies depend on approval and acceptance as much as chameleons, but bullies push others to agree with them rather than their agreeing with others. Disagreement threatens a bully as much as it threatens a chameleon. An extreme rebel is a poorly differentiated person too, but he pretends to be a "self" by routinely opposing the positions of others.

A person with a well-differentiated "self" recognizes his realistic dependence on others, but he can stay calm and clear-headed enough in the face of conflict, criticism, and rejection to distinguish thinking rooted in a careful assessment of the facts from thinking clouded by emotionality. Thoughtfully acquired principles help guide decision-making about important family and social issues, making him less at the mercy of the feelings of the moment. What he decides and what he says matches what he does. He can act selflessly, but his acting in the best interests of the group is a thoughtful choice, not a response to relationship pressures. Confident in his thinking, he can support others' views without being a disciple or reject others' views without polarizing the differences. He defines himself without being pushy and deals with pressure to yield without being wishy-washy.

Every human society has its well-differentiated people, poorly differentiated people, and people at many gradations between these extremes. Consequently, the families and other groups that make up a society differ in the intensity of their emotional interdependence depending on the differentiation levels of their members. The more intense the interdependence, the less a group's capacity to adapt to potentially stressful events without a marked escalation of chronic anxiety. Everyone is subject to problems in his work and personal life, but the greater vulnerability of less differentiated people and families to periods of heightened chronic anxiety contributes to their having a disproportionate share of society's most serious clinical and other life problems.

Example

The example of the Michael-Martha-Amy triangle reflects how a lack of differentiation of self plays out in a family unit, in their case, a moderately differentiated unit. The description that follows is of how this triangle would play out if Michael, Martha, and Amy were more differentiated people.

Michael and Martha were quite happy during the first two years of their marriage. He liked making the major decisions, but did not assume he knew "best." He always told Martha what he was thinking and he listened carefully to her ideas. Their exchanges were usually thoughtful and led to decisions that respected the vital interests of both people. Martha had always been attracted to Michael's sense of responsibility and willingness to make decisions, but she also lived by a principle that she was responsible for thinking things through for herself and telling Michael what she thought. She did not assume Michael usually knew "best."

Analysis: Because the level of stress on a marriage is often less during the early years, particularly before the births of children and the addition of other responsibilities, the less adaptive moderately differentiated marriage and the more adaptive well-differentiated marriage can look similar because the tension level is low. Stress is necessary to expose the limits of a family's adaptive capacity.

Martha conceived during the third year of the marriage and had a fairly smooth pregnancy. She had a few physical problems, but dealt with them with equanimity. She was somewhat anxious about being an adequate mother, but felt she could manage these fears. When she talked to Michael about her fears, she did not expect that he would solve them for her, but she thought more clearly about her fears when she talked them out with him. He listened, but was not patronizing. He recognized his own fears about the coming changes in their lives and acknowledged them to Martha.

Analysis: The stresses associated with the real and anticipated changes of the pregnancy trigger some anxiety in both Michael and Martha, but their interaction does not escalate the anxiety and make it chronic. Martha has somewhat heightened needs and expectations of Michael, but takes responsibility for managing her anxiety and has realistic expectations about what he can do for her. Michael does not get particularly reactive to Martha's expectations and recognizes he is anxious too. Each remains a resource to the other.

A female infant was born after a fairly smooth labor. They named her Amy. Martha weathered the delivery fairly well and was ready to go home when her doctor discharged her. The infant care over the next few months was physically exhausting for Martha, but she was not heavily burdened by anxieties about the baby or about her adequacy as a mother. She continued to talk to Michael about her thoughts and feelings, and still did not feel he was supposed to do something to make her feel better. Michael had increasing work pressures and she understood it. He remained emotionally available to her, even if only by phone at times. He worried about work issues, but did not ruminate about them to Martha. When she asked how it was going, he responded fairly factually and appreciated her interest. He occasionally wished Martha would not get anxious about things, but realized she could manage. He was not compelled to "fix" things for her.

Analysis: Sure of herself as a person, Martha is able to relate to Amy without feeling overwhelmed by responsibilities and demands and without unfounded fears about the child's well-being. Sure of himself, Michael can meet the reality demands of his job without feeling guilty that he is neglecting Martha. Each spouse recognizes the pressure the other is under and neither makes a "federal case" about being neglected. Each is sufficiently confident in the other's loyalty and commitment that neither needs much reassurance about it. By the parents relating comfortably to each other, Amy is not triangled into marital tensions. She does not have a void to fill in her mother's life related to distance between her parents.

After a few months, Michael and Martha were able to find time to do some things by themselves. Martha found that her anxieties about being a mother toned down and she did not worry much about Amy. As Amy grew, Martha did not perceive her as an insecure child that needed special attention. She was positive about Amy, but not constantly praising her in the name of reinforcing Amy's self-image. Michael and Martha discussed their thoughts and feelings about Amy, but they were not preoccupied with her. They were pleased to have her and took pleasure in watching her develop.

Amy grew to be a responsible young child. She sensed the limits of what was realistic for her parents to do for her and respected those limits. There were few demands and no tantrums. Michael did not feel critical of Amy very often and Martha did not defend Amy to him when he was critical. Martha figured Michael and Amy could manage their relationship. Amy seemed equally comfortable with both of her parents and relished exploring her environment.

Analysis: Michael and Martha can see Amy as a separate and distinct person. The beginning differentiation between Amy and her parents is evident when Amy is a young child. They have adapted quite successfully to the anxieties they each experienced associated with the addition of a child and the increased demands in Michael's work life. Their high levels of differentiation allow the three of them to be in close contact with little triangling.

The concept of the *nuclear family emotional system* describes four basic relationship patterns that govern where problems develop in a family. People's attitudes and beliefs about relationships play a role in the patterns, but the forces primarily driving them are part of the emotional system. The patterns operate in intact, single-parent, step-parent, and other nuclear family configurations.

Clinical problems or symptoms usually develop during periods of heightened and prolonged family tension. The tension level depends on the stress a family encounters, how a family adapts to stress, and on a family's connection with extended family and social networks. Tension increases the activity of one or more of the four relationship patterns. Where symptoms develop depends on which patterns are most active. The higher the tension, the more chance that symptoms will be severe and that several people will be symptomatic.

The four basic relationship patterns are:

Marital conflict: As family tension increases and the spouses get more anxious, each spouse externalizes his or her anxiety into the marital relationship. Each focuses on what is wrong with the other, each tries to control the other, and each resists the other's efforts at control.

Dysfunction in one spouse: One spouse pressures the other to think and act in certain ways and the other yields to the pressure. Both spouses accommodate to preserve harmony, but one does more of it. The interaction is comfortable for both people up to a point, but if family tension rises further, the subordinate spouse may yield so much self-control that his or her anxiety increases significantly. The anxiety fuels, if other necessary factors are present, the development of a psychiatric, medical, or social dysfunction.

Impairment of one or more children: The spouses focus their anxieties on one or more of their children. They worry excessively about the child and usually have an idealized or negative view of him. The more the parents focus on the child the more the child focuses on them. He is more reactive than his siblings to the parents' attitudes, needs, and expectations. The process undercuts the child's differentiation from the family and makes him vulnerable to act out or internalize family tensions. The child's anxiety can impair school performance, social relationships, and even his health.

Emotional distance: This pattern is consistently associated with the others. People distance from each other to reduce relationship intensity, but at the risk of becoming too isolated.

The basic relationship patterns result in family tensions coming to rest in certain parts of the family. The more anxiety one person or one relationship absorbs, the less other people must absorb. This means that some family members maintain their functioning at the expense of others. People do not want to hurt each other, but when anxiety chronically dictates behavior, someone usually suffers for it.

Example

Returning to the parental triangle example of Michael, Martha, and Amy to illustrate the nuclear family emotional system concept, the tensions generated by Michael and Martha's interactions lead to emotional distance between them and to an anxious focus on Amy. Amy reacts to her parents' emotional overinvolvement with her by making immature demands on them, particularly on her mother.

Analysis: A parent's emotional overinvolvement with a child programs the child to be as emotionally focused on the parent as the parent is on the child and to react intensely to real or imagined signs of withdrawal by the parent.

When Amy was four years old, Martha got pregnant again. She wanted another child, but soon began to worry about whether she could meet the emotional needs of two children. Would Amy be harmed by feeling left out? Martha worried about telling Amy that she would soon have a little brother or sister, wanting to put off dealing with her anticipated reaction as long as possible. Michael thought it was silly, but went along with Martha. He was outwardly supportive about the pregnancy, he too wanted another child, but he worried about Martha's coping abilities.

Analysis: Martha externalizes her anxiety onto Amy rather than onto her husband or rather than internalizing it. Michael avoids conflict with Martha by supporting the focus on Amy and avoids dealing with his own anxieties by focusing on Martha's coping abilities.

Apart from her fairly intense anxieties about Amy, Martha's second pregnancy was easier than the first. A daughter, Marie, was born without complications. This time Michael took more time away from work to help at home, feeling and seeing that Martha seemed "on the edge." He took over many household duties and was even more directive of Martha. Martha was obsessed with Amy feeling displaced by Marie and gave in even more to Amy's demands for attention. Martha and Amy began to get into struggles over how available Martha could be to her. When Michael would get home at night, he would take Amy off her mother's hands and entertain her. He also began feeling neglected himself and quite disappointed in Martha's lack of coping skills.

Martha had done some drinking before she married Michael and after Amy was born, but stopped completely during the pregnancy with Marie. When Marie was a few months old, however, Martha began drinking again, mostly wine during the evenings, and much more than in the past. She somewhat tried to cover up the amount of drinking she did, feeling Michael would be critical of it. He was. He accused her of not trying, not caring, and being selfish. Martha felt he was right. She felt less and less able to make decisions and more and more dependent on Michael. She felt he deserved better, but also resented his criticism and patronizing. She drank more, even during the day. Michael began calling her an alcoholic.

Analysis: The pattern of sickness in a spouse has emerged, with Martha as the one making the most adjustments in her functioning to preserve harmony in the marriage. It is easier for Martha to be the problem than to stand up to Michael's diagnosing her and, besides, she feels she really is the problem. As the pattern unfolds, Michael increasingly overfunctions and Martha increasingly underfunctions. Michael is as allergic to conflict as Martha is, opting to function for her rather than risk the disharmony he would trigger by expecting her to function more responsibly.

By the time Amy and Marie were both in school, Martha reached a serious low point. She felt worthless and out of control. She felt Michael did everything, but that she could not talk to him. Her doctor was concerned about her physical health. Finally, Martha confided in him about the extent of her drinking. Michael had been pushing her to get help, but Martha had reached a point of resisting almost all of Michael's directives. However, her doctor scared her and she decided to go to Alcoholics Anonymous.

Martha felt completely accepted by the A.A. group and greatly relieved to tell her story. She stopped drinking almost immediately and developed a very close connection to her sponsor, an older woman. She felt she could be herself with the people at A.A. in a way she could not be with Michael. She began to function much better at home, began a part-time job, but also attended A.A. meetings frequently. Michael had complained bitterly about her drinking, but now he complained about her preoccupation with her new found A.A. friends. Martha gained a certain strength from her new friends and was encouraged by them "to stand up" to Michael. She did. They began fighting frequently. Martha felt more like herself again. Michael was bitter.

Analysis: Martha's involvement with A.A. helped her stop drinking, but it did not solve the family problem. The level of family tension has not changed and the emotional distance in the marriage has not changed. Because of "borrowing strength" from her A.A. group, Martha is more inclined to fight with Michael than to go along and internalize the anxiety. This means the marital pattern has shifted somewhat from dysfunction in a spouse to marital conflict, but the family has not changed in a basic way. In other words, Martha's level of differentiation of self has not changed through her A.A. involvement, but her functioning has improved.

Family Projection Process

The *family projection process* describes the primary way parents transmit their emotional problems to a child. The projection process can impair the functioning of one or more children and increase their vulnerability to clinical symptoms. Children inherit many types of problems (as well as strengths) through the relationships with their parents, but the problems they inherit that most affect their lives are relationship sensitivities such as heightened needs for attention and approval, difficulty dealing with expectations, the tendency to blame oneself or others, feeling responsible for the happiness of others or that others are responsible for one's own happiness, and acting impulsively to relieve the anxiety of the moment rather than tolerating anxiety and acting thoughtfully. If the projection process is fairly intense, the child develops stronger relationship sensitivities than his parents. The sensitivities increase a person's vulnerability to symptoms by fostering behaviors that escalate chronic anxiety in a relationship system.

The projection process follows three steps: (1) the parent focuses on a child out of fear that something is wrong with the child; (2) the parent interprets the child's behavior as confirming the fear; and (3) the parent treats the child as if something is really wrong with child. These steps of scanning, diagnosing, and treating begin early in the child's life and continue. The parents' fears and perceptions so shape the child's development and behavior that he grows to embody their fears and perceptions. One reason the projection process is a self-fulfilling prophecy is that parents try to "fix" the problem they have diagnosed in the child; for example, parents perceive their child to have a low self-esteem, they repeatedly try to affirm the child, and the child's self-esteem grows dependent on their affirmation.

Parents often feel they have not given enough love, attention, or support to a child manifesting problems, but they have invested more time, energy, and worry in this child than in his siblings. The siblings less involved in the family projection process have a more mature and reality-based relationship with their parents that fosters the siblings developing into less needy, less reactive, and more goal-directed people.

Both parents participate equally in the family projection process, but in different ways. The mother is usually the primary caretaker and more prone than the father to excessive emotional involvement with one or more of the children. The father typically occupies the outside position in the parental triangle, except during periods of heightened tension in the mother-child relationship. Both parents are unsure of themselves in relationship to the child, but commonly one parent acts sure of himself or herself and the other parent goes along. The intensity of projection process is unrelated to the amount of time parents spend with a child.

Example

The case of Michael, Martha, and Amy illustrates the family projection process. Martha's anxiety about Amy began before Amy was born. Martha feared she would transfer inadequacies she had felt as a child, and still felt, to her own child. This was one reason Martha had mixed feelings about being a mother.

Like many parents, Martha felt a mother's most important task was to make a child feel loved. In the name of showing love, she was acutely responsive to Amy's desires for attention. If Amy seemed bored and out of sorts, Martha was there with an idea or plan. She believed a child's road to confidence and independence was in the child feeling secure about herself. Martha did not recognize how sensitive she was to any sign in Amy that she might be upset or troubled and how quickly she would move in to fix the problem.

Martha loved Amy deeply. She and Amy often seemed like one person in the way they were attuned to each other. As a very small toddler, Amy was as sensitive to her mother's moods and wants as Martha was to Amy's moods and wants.

Analysis: Martha's excessive involvement programs Amy to want much of her mother's attention and to be highly sensitive to her mother's emotional state. Both mother and child act to reinforce the intense connection between them.

At some point in the unfolding of their relationship, Martha began to feel irritated at times by what Martha regarded as Amy's "insatiable need" for attention. Martha would try to distance from Amy's neediness, but not very successfully because Amy had ways to involve her mother with her. Martha flip-flopped between pleading with and cajoling Amy one minute and being angry at and directive of her the next. It seemed to lock them together even more tightly. Martha looked to Michael to take over at such times. Despite calling Amy's need for attention insatiable, Martha felt Amy really needed more of her time and she faulted herself for not being able to give enough. She wanted Michael to help with the task. It bothered Martha if Amy seemed upset with her. Amy's upsets triggered guilt in Martha and a fear that they were no longer close companions. She wanted to soothe Amy and feel close to her.

Analysis: Martha blames Amy for the demands she makes on her, but at the same time feels she is failing Amy. Martha tries to "fix" Amy's problem by doing more of what she has already been doing and solicits Michael's help in it. Martha is meeting many of her own needs for emotional closeness and companionship through Amy, thus gets very distressed if Amy seems unhappy with her. The marital distance accentuates Martha's need for Amy.

Martha's second pregnancy changed a reasonably manageable situation into an unmanageable one. The dilemma of meeting the needs of both children seemed impossible to Martha. She felt Amy was already showing signs of "inheriting" her insecurities. How had she failed her?

When it was time for Amy to start school, Martha sought long conferences with the kindergarten teacher to plan the transition. If Amy balked at going to school, Martha became frightened, angry, exasperated, and guilty. The kindergarten teacher felt she understood children like Amy and took great interest in her. Amy was bright, thrived on the teacher's attention, and performed very well in school. Martha had none of these fears when Marie started school and, not surprisingly, none of the school transition problems occurred with her. Marie did not seem to require so much of the teacher's attention; she just pursued her interests.

As Amy progressed through grade school, her adjustment to school seemed to depend heavily on the teacher she had in a particular year. If the teacher seemed to take an unusual interest in her, she performed very well, but if the teacher treated her as one of the group, she would lose interest in her work. Martha focused on making sure Amy got the "right" teacher whenever possible. Marie's performance did not depend on a particular teacher.

Analysis: Martha's difficulty being a "self" with her children is reflected in her feeling inordinately responsible for the happiness of both children. This makes it extremely difficult for her to interact comfortably with two children. Amy transfers the relationship intensity she has with her mother to her teachers. When a teacher makes her special, Amy performs very well, but without that type of relationship, Amy performs less well. Marie is less involved with her mother and, consequently, her performance is less dependent on the relationship environment at school and at home.

If Amy complained about the ways other kids treated her in school, Martha and Michael would talk to her about not being so sensitive, tell her she should not care so much about what other people think. If Amy had a special friend, she was extremely sensitive to that friend paying attention to another little girl. Martha lectured Amy about being less sensitive, but also planned outings and parties designed to help Amy with her friendships. Michael criticized Martha for this, saying Amy should work out these problems for herself, but he basically went along with all of Martha's frenzied efforts.

Analysis: The parents' words do not match their actions. They lecture Amy about being less sensitive, but the frequent lectures belie their own anxieties about such issues and their doubts about Amy's ability to cope. Amy's sensitivity to being in the outside position in a triangle with her playmates reflects her programming for such relationship sensitivities in the parental triangle.

Martha and Amy had turmoil in their relationship during Amy's elementary school years, but things got worse in middle school. Amy began having academic problems and complained about feeling lost in the larger school. She seemed unhappy to Martha. Martha talked to Michael and to the pediatrician about getting therapy for Amy. They hired tutors for Amy in two of her subjects, even though they knew that part of the problem was Amy not working hard in those subjects. When Amy's grades did not improve, Michael criticized her for not taking advantage of the help they were giving and not appreciating them as parents. Martha scolded Michael for being too hard on Amy, but inwardly she felt even more critical of her than Michael did. She had worked hard to prevent these very problems in Amy. How could Amy disappoint her so much? In the summers when there were no academic pressures, Martha and Amy got along much better.

Analysis: Commonly parents get critical of a child with whom they have been excessively involved if the child's performance drops. They push for the child to have therapy or tutors rather than think about the changes they themselves need to make. Medicine, psychiatry, and the larger society usually reinforce the child focus by defining the problem as in the child and by often implying that the parents are not attentive and caring enough.

The big changes occurred when Amy started high school. Martha felt Amy was telling her less of what was happening in her life and that she was more sullen and withdrawn. Amy also had a new group of girlfriends that seemed less desirable to Martha. Amy had also found boys. Martha and Amy got into more frequent conflicts. Amy felt controlled by her parents, not given the freedom to make her own decisions, pick her own friends. She resented her mother's obvious intrusions into her room when she was out. She began lying to her mother in an effort to evade her rules. Martha was no longer drinking herself at this point, but worried that Amy was using drugs and alcohol. She challenged Amy about it, but her challenges were met with denials.

When Martha felt particularly overwhelmed by the situation, Michael would step in and try to lay down the law to Amy. He accused Amy of not appreciating all they had done for her and of deliberately trying to hurt them. He wanted to know "why" she disobeyed them. Amy would lash back at her father in these discussions, at which point Martha would intervene. Amy stayed away from the house more, told her parents less and less, and got in with a fairly wild crowd. She acted out some of her parents' worst fears, but did not feel particularly good about herself and about what she was doing. Amy felt alienated from her parents. The parents' focus on her deteriorating grades included lectures and groundings, but Amy easily evaded these efforts to control and change her.

Analysis: The more intense the family projection process has been, the more intense the adolescent rebellion. Parents typically blame the rebellion on adolescence, but the parents reactivity to the child fuels the rebellion as much as the child's reactivity. When the parents demand to know "why" Amy acts as she does, they place the problem in Amy. Similarly, parents often blame the influence of the peer group, which also places the problem outside themselves. Peers are an important influence, but a child's vulnerability to peer pressure is related to the intensity of the family process. The intense family process closes down communication and isolates Amy from the family. This is why a child who is very intensely connected to her parents can feel distant from them. The siblings who are less involved in the family problem navigate adolescence more smoothly.

Michael and Martha became increasingly critical of Amy, but also latched onto any signs she might be doing a little better. They gave her her own phone, bought the clothes she "just had to have," and gave her a car for her sixteenth birthday. Many of these things were done in the name of making Amy feel special and important, hoping that would motivate her to do better. Throughout all the turmoil surrounding Amy, Marie presented few problems.

Analysis: The parents' permissiveness is just as important in perpetuating the problems in Amy as the critical focus on her. As a teenager, Amy is just as critical of her parents as they are of her. Marie is a more mature person than Amy, but she is not free of the family problem; for example, she sides with her parents in blaming Amy for the family turmoil.

T he concept of the *multigenerational transmission process* describes how small differences in the levels of differentiation between parents and their offspring and between the members of a sibling group lead over many generations to marked differences in differentiation among the members of a multigenerational family. The information creating these differences is transmitted across generations through relationships. The transmission occurs on several interconnected levels ranging from the conscious teaching and learning of information to the automatic and unconscious programming of emotional reactions and behaviors. Relationally and genetically transmitted information interact to shape an individual's "self."

The combination of parents actively shaping the development of their offspring, offspring innately responding to their parents' moods, attitudes, and actions, and the long dependency period of human offspring results in people developing levels of differentiation of self similar to their parents' levels. However, the relationship patterns of nuclear family emotional systems often result in at least one member of a sibling group developing a little more "self" and another member developing a little less "self" than the parents.

The next step in the multigenerational transmission process is people predictably selecting mates with levels of differentiation of self that match their own. Therefore, if one sibling's level of "self" is higher and another sibling's level of "self" is lower than that of the parents, one sibling's marriage is more differentiated and the other sibling's marriage is less differentiated than the parents' marriage. If each sibling then has a child who is more differentiated and a child who is less differentiated than himself, one three-generational line becomes progressively more differentiated (the most differentiated child of the most differentiated sibling) and one line becomes progressively less differentiated (the least differentiated child of the least differentiated sibling). As these processes repeat over multiple generations, the differences between family lines grow increasingly marked.

Level of differentiation of self can affect longevity, marital stability, reproduction, health, educational accomplishments, and occupational successes. This impact of differentiation on overall life functioning explains the marked variation that typically exists in the lives of the members of a multigenerational family. The highly differentiated people have unusually stable nuclear families and contribute much to society; the poorly differentiated people have chaotic personal lives and depend heavily on others to sustain them. A key implication of the multigenerational concept is that the roots of the most severe human problems as well as of the highest levels of human adaptation are generations deep.

The multigenerational transmission process not only programs the levels of "self" people develop, but it also programs how people interact with others. Both types of programming affect the selection of a spouse. For example, if a family programs someone to attach intensely to others and to function in a helpless and indecisive way, he will likely select a mate who not only attaches to him with equal intensity, but one who directs others and makes decisions for them.

Example

The multigenerational transmission process helps explain the particular patterns that have played out in the nuclear family of Michael, Martha, Amy, and Marie. Martha is the youngest of three daughters from an intact Midwestern family. From her teen years on, Martha did not feel especially close to either of her parents, but especially to her mother. She experienced her mother as competent and caring, but often intrusive in her affairs and critical. Martha felt she could not please her mother.

Her sisters seemed to feel more secure and competent than Martha. She asked herself how she could grow up in a seemingly "normal" family and have so many problems, and answered herself that there must be something wrong with her. When she faced important dilemmas in her life and had decisions to make, her mother got involved and strongly influenced Martha's choices. Her mother said Martha should make her own decisions, but her mother's actions did not match her words. One of her mother's biggest fears was that Martha would make the wrong decision. In time, Martha's sisters came to view her much like her mother did and treated her as the baby of the family, as one needing special guidance. Martha's father was sympathetic with her one-down position in the family, but distanced from family tensions.

Martha detested herself for needing the acceptance and approval of others to function effectively and for feeling she could not act more independently. She worried about making the wrong decision and turned frequently to her mother for help.

Analysis: The primary relationship pattern in Martha's family of origin was impairment of one or more children and the projection process focused primarily on Martha. The mother's overfunctioning promoted Martha's underfunctioning, but Martha largely blamed herself for her difficulties making decisions and functioning independently. Martha's intense need for approval and acceptance reflected the high level of involvement with her mother. She managed the intensity with her mother with emotional distance. These basic patterns were later replicated in her marriage and with Amy.

Martha's mother is the oldest child in her family and functioned as a second parent to her three younger siblings. Martha's mother's mother became a chronic invalid after her last child was born. As a child, Martha's mother functioned as a second mother in her family and, with the encouragement of her father, did much of the caretaking of her invalid mother. Martha's mother basked in the approval she gained from both of her parents, especially from her father. Her father was often critical of his wife, insisting she could do more for herself if she would try. Martha's grandmother responded to the criticism by taking to bed, often for days at a time. Martha's mother learned to thrive on taking care of others and being needed.

Analysis: Martha's mother probably had almost as intense an involvement with her parents as she subsequently had with Martha, but the styles of the involvements were different. Two relationship patterns dominated Martha's mother's nuclear family: dysfunction in one spouse and overinvolvement with a child. Martha's mother was intensely involved in the triangles with her parents and younger siblings and in the position of overfunctioning for others. In other words, she learned to meet her strongly programmed needs for emotional closeness by taking care of others, a pattern that played out with Martha.

Michael grew up as an only child in an intact family from the Pacific Northwest. He met Martha when he attended college in the Midwest. Michael's mother began having frequent bouts of serious depression about the time he started grade school. She was twice hospitalized psychiatrically, once after an overdose of tranquilizers.

Michael felt "allergic" to his mother's many problems and kept his distance from her, especially during his adolescence. He cared about her and felt she would help him in any way she could, but viewed her as helpless and incompetent. He resented her "not trying harder." He had a reasonably comfortable relationship with his father, but felt his father made the family situation worse by opting for "peace at any price." It was easier for his father to give in to his wife's sometimes childish demands than to draw a line with her. Michael related to his mother almost exactly like his father did. His mother expressed resentment about her husband's passivity. She accused him of not really caring about her, only doing things for her because she demanded it. Michael's mother worshiped Michael and was jealous of interests and people that took him away from her.

Analysis: Interestingly, Michael's parental triangle was similar to Martha's mother's parental triangle. His mother was intensely involved with him and it programmed Michael both to need this level of emotional support from the important female in his life, but also to react critically to the female's neediness. Michael's parental triangle also fostered a belief that he knew best.

Michael's mother had been a "star" in her family when she was growing up. She was an excellent student and athlete. She had a very conflictual relationship with her mother and an idealized view of her father. She met Michael's father when they were both in college. He was two years older than she and when he graduated, she quit school to marry him. Her parents were very upset about the decision. Michael's father had been at loose ends when he met his future wife, but she was what he needed. He built a very successful business career with her emotional support. His functioning was higher in his work life than in his family life.

Analysis: Michael's father functioned on a higher level in his business life than in his family life, a discrepancy that is commonly present in people with mid-range levels of differentiation of self.

6 Emotional Cutoff

The concept of *emotional cutoff* describes people managing their unresolved emotional issues with parents, siblings, and other family members by reducing or totally cutting off emotional contact with them. Emotional contact can be reduced by people moving away from their families and rarely going home, or it can be reduced by people staying in physical contact with their families but avoiding sensitive issues. Relationships may look "better" if people cut off to manage them, but the problems are dormant and not resolved.

People reduce the tensions of family interactions by cutting off, but risk making their new relationships too important. For example, the more a man cuts off from his family of origin, the more he looks to his spouse, children, and friends to meet his needs. This makes him vulnerable to pressuring them to be certain ways for him or accommodating too much to their expectations of him out of fear of jeopardizing the relationship. New relationships are typically smooth in the beginning, but the patterns people are trying to escape eventually emerge and generate tensions. People who are cut off may try to stabilize their intimate relationships by creating substitute "families" with social and work relationships.

Everyone has some degree of unresolved attachment to his or her original family, but well-differentiated people have much more resolution than less differentiated people. An unresolved attachment can take many forms. For example, (1) a person feels more like a child when he is home and looks to his parents to make decisions for him that he can make for himself, or (2) a person feels guilty when he is in more contact with his parents and feels he must solve their conflicts or distresses, or (3) a person feels enraged that his parents do not seem to understand or approve of him. An unresolved attachment relates to the immaturity of both the parents and the adult child, but people typically blame themselves or others for the problems.

People often look forward to going home, hoping things will be different this time, but the old interactions usually surface within hours. It may take the form of surface harmony with powerful emotional undercurrents or it may deteriorate into shouting matches and hysterics. Both the person and his family may feel exhausted even after a brief visit. It may be easier for the parents if an adult child keeps his distance. The family gets so anxious and reactive when he is home that they are relieved when he leaves. The siblings of a highly cut off member often get furious at him when he is home and blame him for upsetting the parents. People do not want it to be this way, but the sensitivities of all parties preclude comfortable contact.

Example

Neither Michael nor Martha wanted to live near their families. When Michael got a good job offer on the East coast, both of them were eager to move east. They told their families they were moving away because of Michael's great job offer, but they welcomed the physical distance from their families. Michael felt guilty about living far away from his parents, and his parents were upset about it, especially Michael's mother. Michael called home every weekend and managed to combine business trips with brief stays with his parents. He did not look forward to the phone calls and usually felt depressed after them. He felt as if his mother deliberately put him on "guilt trips" by emphasizing how poorly she was doing and how much she missed seeing him. She never failed to ask if his company could transfer him closer to home. It was much less depressing for Michael to talk to his father,

but they talked mostly about Michael's job and what his Dad was doing in retirement.

*Analysis: Michael blamed his mother for the problems in their
relationship and, despite his guilt, felt justified distancing from her.
People commonly have a "stickier" unresolved emotional attachment
with their mothers than with their fathers because the way a parental
triangle usually operates is that the mother is too involved with the
child and the father is in the outside position.*

In the early years, Martha would sometimes participate in Michael's
phone calls home but, as her problems mounted, she usually left the
calls to Michael. Michael did not say much to his parents about Martha's
drinking or about the tensions in their marriage. He would report on
how the kids were doing. Michael, Martha, and the kids usually made
one visit to Michael's parents each year. They did not look forward to
the four days they would spend there, but Michael's mother thrived on
having them. Martha never said anything to Michael's parents about
her drinking or the marital tensions, but she talked at length about Amy
to Michael's mother. Amy often developed middle ear infections during or soon after these trips.

*Analysis: Frequently one or more family members get sick lead-
ing up to, during, or soon after trips home. Amy was more vulnerable
because of the anxious focus on her.*

Martha followed a pattern similar to Michael's in dealing with her
family. One difference was that her parents came east fairly often.
When they came, Martha's mother would get more worried about Martha
and critical of both her drinking and of how she was raising Amy. Martha
dreaded these exchanges with her mother and complained to Michael
for days after her parents returned home. Deep down, however, Martha
felt her mother was right about her deficiencies. Martha's mother
pumped Michael for information about Martha when Martha was

reluctant to talk. Michael was all too willing to discuss Martha's perceived shortcomings with her mother.

Analysis: Given the striking parallels between the unresolved issues in Michael's relationship with his family, Martha's relationship with her family, and the issues in their marriage, emotional cutoff clearly did not solve any problems. It simply shifted the problems to their marital relationship and to Amy.

Sibling Position

B owen theory incorporates the research of psychologist Walter Toman as a foundation for its concept of *sibling position.* Bowen observed the impact of sibling position on development and behavior in his family research. However, he found Toman's work so thorough and consistent with his ideas that he incorporated it into his theory.

The basic idea is that people who grow up in the same sibling position predictably have important common characteristics. For example, oldest children tend to gravitate to leadership positions and youngest children often prefer to be followers. The characteristics of one position are not "better" than those of another position, but are complementary. For example, a boss who is an oldest child may work unusually well with a first assistant who is a youngest child. Youngest children may like to be in charge, but their leadership style typically differs from an oldest's style.

Toman's research showed that spouses' sibling positions affect the chance of their divorcing. For example, if an older brother of a younger sister marries a younger sister of an older brother, less chance of a divorce exists than if an older brother of a brother marries an older sister of a sister. The sibling or rank positions are complementary in the first case and each spouse is familiar with living with someone of the opposite sex. In the second case, however, the rank positions are not complementary and neither spouse grew up with a member of the opposite sex. An older brother of a brother and an older sister of a sister are prone to battle over who is in charge; two youngest children are prone to struggle over who gets to lean on whom.

People in the same sibling position, of course, exhibit marked differences in functioning. The concept of differentiation can explain some of the differences. For example, rather than being comfortable with responsibility and leadership, an oldest child who is anxiously focused on may grow up to be markedly indecisive and highly reactive to expectations. Consequently, his younger brother may become a "functional oldest," filling a void in the family system. He is the chronologically younger child, but develops more characteristics of an oldest child than his older brother. A youngest child who is anxiously focused on may become an unusually helpless and demanding person. In contrast, two mature youngest children may cooperate extremely effectively in a marriage and be at very low risk for a divorce.

Middle children exhibit the functional characteristics of two sibling positions. For example, if a girl has an older brother and a younger sister, she usually has some of the characteristics of both a younger sister of a brother and an older sister of a sister. The sibling positions of a person's parents are also important to consider. An oldest child whose parents are both youngests encounters a different set of parental expectations than an oldest child whose parents are both oldests.

Example

Knowledge of Michael and Martha's sibling positions and those of their parents adds to the understanding of how things played out in their lives. Martha is the youngest of three girls and was the most intensely focused on child in her family. Furthermore, Martha's mother is the oldest of four siblings and was raised in a family with a mother who was a chronic invalid. Martha's mother was a not very well differentiated oldest daughter. Her life energy focused on taking care of and directing others to the point that she unwittingly undermined the functioning of her youngest daughter. Martha played out the opposite side of the problem by becoming an indecisive, helpless, and mostly self-blaming person. Martha's father was the youngest brother in a family of five children.

Analysis: Martha, by virtue of her mother's focus on her, has the moderately exaggerated traits of a youngest child. Furthermore, her father being a youngest and her mother an oldest favored her mother's functioning setting the tone in the family. In other words, her mother was quicker to act than her father in face of problems.

Michael is an only child who, like Martha's mother, was raised in a family with a mother who had many problems. Michael's father is the younger brother of a sister and his mother is the older sister of a brother. Michael's mother was the child more focused on when she was growing up, a focus that took the form of high performance expectations coupled with considerable family anxiety about her ability to meet those expectations. In many ways, Michael's father was quite dependent on his wife for affirmation and direction, even when she was depressed and overwhelmed. As an only child, the pattern of functioning of the triangle with his parents was the major influence on Michael's development. His emotional programming in that triangle made him a perfect fit with Martha.

Analysis: Michael's only child position makes him a somewhat reluctant leader in his nuclear family. He wants Martha to function better and to take more responsibility. He is unhappy feeling the pressure himself. Despite being in the one-up position in the marriage, he is as dependent on Martha as his father was dependent on his wife.

E ach concept in Bowen theory applies to nonfamily groups, such as work and social organizations. The concept of *societal emotional process* describes how the emotional system governs behavior on a societal level, promoting both progressive and regressive periods in a society. Cultural forces are important in how a society functions but are insufficient for explaining the ebb and flow in how well societies adapt to the challenges that face them.

Bowen's first clue about parallels between familial and societal emotional functioning came from treating families with juvenile delinquents. The parents in such families give the message, "We love you no matter what you do." Despite impassioned lectures about responsibility and sometimes harsh punishments, the parents give in to the child more than they hold the line. The child rebels against the parents and is adept at sensing the uncertainty of their positions. The child feels controlled and lies to get around the parents. He is indifferent to their punishments. The parents try to control the child but are largely ineffectual.

Bowen discovered that during the 1960s the courts became more like the parents of delinquents. Many in the juvenile court system considered the delinquent as a victim of bad parents. They tried to understand him and often reduced the consequences of his actions in the hope of effecting a change in his behavior. If the delinquent became a frequent offender, the legal system, much like the parents, expressed its disappointment and imposed harsh penalties. This recognition of a change in one societal institution led Bowen to notice that similar changes were occurring in other institutions, such as in schools and governments.

The downward spiral in families dealing with delinquency is an anxiety-driven regression in functioning. In a regression, people act to relieve the anxiety of the moment rather than act on principle and a long-term view. A regressive pattern began unfolding in society after World War II. It worsened some during the 1950s and rapidly intensified during the 1960s. The "symptoms" of societal regression include a growth of crime and violence, an increasing divorce rate, a more litigious attitude, a greater polarization between racial groups, less principled decision-making by leaders, the drug abuse epidemic, an increase in bankruptcy, and a focus on rights over responsibilities.

Human societies undergo periods of regression and progression in their history. The current regression seems related to factors such as the population explosion, a sense of diminishing frontiers, and the depletion of natural resources. Bowen predicted that the current regression would, like a family in a regression, continue until the repercussions stemming from taking the easy way out on tough issues exceeded the pain associated with acting on a long-term view. He predicted that will occur before the middle of the twenty-first century and should result in human beings living in more harmony with nature.

Example

It is more difficult for families to raise children in a period of societal regression than in a calmer period. A loosening of standards in society makes it more difficult for less differentiated parents like Michael and Martha to hold a line with their children. The grade inflation in many school systems makes it easier for students to earn passing grades with less work. In the litigious climate, if schools try to hold the line on what they can realistically do for their students, they often face lawsuits from irate parents. The prevalence of drug and alcohol abuse gives parents more things to worry about with their adolescents.

The current societal regression is characterized by an increased child focus in the culture. Much anxiety exists about the future generation. Parents are criticized for being too busy with their own pursuits to be adequately available to their children, both to support them and to monitor their activities. When children like Amy report that they feel distant from their parents and alienated from their values, the parents' critics fail to appreciate the emotional intensity that generates such alienation. The critics prod the parents to do more of what they have already been doing.

People who advocate more focus on the children cite the many problems young people are having as justification for their position. Using the child's problems as justification for increasing the focus on them is precisely what the child-focused parents have been doing all along. An increase in the problems young people are having is part of an emotional process in society *as a whole*. A more constructive direction would be for people to examine their own contributions to societal regression and to work on themselves rather than tofocus on improving the future generation.